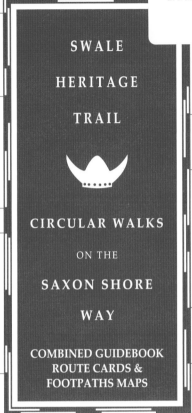

SWALE

HERITAGE

TRAIL

CIRCULAR WALKS

ON THE

SAXON SHORE

WAY

**COMBINED GUIDEBOOK
ROUTE CARDS &
FOOTPATHS MAPS**

WELCOME TO THE GARDEN OF ENGLAND

Produced by Countryside Group,
Kent County Council, Planning Department.

Designed by The Design Studio, Kent County Council.

Maps produced by The Design Studio, Kent County Council.

Maps produced with the sanction of the controller of HM
Stationery Office. Crown Copyright reserved.

Printed in Great Britain by County Print, Kent County Council.

Published by Kent County Council, Planning Department,
Springfield, Maidstone, Kent, ME14 2LX.

First published June 1995

Copyright © 1995 Kent County Council

ISBN 1 873010 50 8

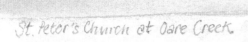

St. Peter's Church at Oare Creek.

CONTENTS

The route cards inside contain the route maps and information about the routes, waymarking, transport, useful addresses and telephone numbers, other walking opportunities, together with some walking advice.

To the best of our knowledge the historical content and all other information is believed to be correct. We should be grateful if you would inform us of any changes, omissions or errors, so that modifications can be made in subsequent revisions of the book.

INTRODUCTION

The Swale Heritage Trail is the third in a series of walks linked to the Saxon Shore Way in series with the Shorne and Higham Marshes, and Brockhill Walks. Other routes are planned and in preparation.

The concept of a Heritage Trail has arisen from the uniqueness of the north Kent Marshes within South-East England and the desire of visitors to know more about the area.

The trail outlined in this brochure traverses an area within the marshes which has been least effected by changes and industrialisation over the last century. It is an area between Sittingbourne and Faversham, two contrasting towns today but whose old industries have historically been built upon each town's access to the sea via two creeks, Milton Creek and Faversham Creek. It is these creeks and the towns themselves that provide borders to the trail detailed. To the south, the area is bordered by Watling Street, the ancient road between London and Dover (the A2).

The Swale is that portion of the Medway estuary that divides the mainland from the Isle of Sheppey. It is designated as a Site of Special Scientific Interest (SSSI) primarily in recognition of its high wading bird population. This conservation value has been further emphasised following designation of the marshlands as an Environmentally Sensitive Area (ESA). This allows farmers to take advantage of special subsidies which are provided when they manage the land in a way that will conserve the wildlife habitats.

Topographically the area is similar to the north Kent Marshes as a whole. The trail passes over land which is no more than 10 metres above sea level and is either level or gently sloping. Annual rainfall is low (500-600mm per year), summers are warm (average 17°c in July) and winters mild (average 4°c in January), but the whole area is exposed to onshore winds. There are some areas of sands and gravel but most of the geology of the area is dominated by clays and alluvium. Consequently many of the soils are heavy. Around 45% of agricultural land is grassland (mostly permanent pasture) and 50% arable.

Side gate to Davington Priory

SAXON SHORE WAY

The Swale Heritage Trail links with part of the Saxon Shore Way, a long distance route which traces the old shore line from Gravesend on the Thames estuary to Rye on the Kent-Sussex border. The name 'Saxon Shore' comes from a series of fortifications built by the Romans, mainly in the late-fourth century, to defend the country against raids by Saxon pirates in the English Channel and the North Sea areas.

Situated at the mouths of the main rivers, these forts contained troops and a fleet to give chase to the marauders and provided a frontier between the civilised and the barbarian world. The Saxon Shore Way passes four of these old forts along the way, Reculver, Richborough, Dover and Lympne, as well as many other places of historic interest, including Rochester and Sandwich. While the coastline has receded in several places, you find estuary and sea views for much of the way. The entire footpath runs for 140 miles.

NATURAL HISTORY

The Trail passes through attractive landscape features with orchards, grazing meadows, farmyards and small villages, so typical of the old Kentish countryside. Relics of some of the old industries of the area also remain, including old brickfields, clay pits and gravel pits. Today many of these pits have become lagoons rich in wildlife.

The coastal paths also look across freshwater grazing marshes with their drainage dykes and wet splashes in winter. Areas of saltmarsh are also present along the Swale channel.

Most of the coastal area is of outstanding wildlife value and has been identified as a Site of Special Scientific Interest. The saltmarshes, mudflats and open estuary have been declared internationally important for birds. Part of the Swale estuary is also designated a Local Nature Reserve.

There are also nature reserves managed by the Kent Trust for Nature Conservation on both sides of Faversham Creek and another near Oare village.

Geology
The soils of the area are formed from Palaeocene sands and gravels of the Thanet formation, with marine alluvial sediments derived from the old Thames basin. Gravel beds were also formed in old, dried up, river beds. Extensive pockets of brickearth are also found.

Wildlife
The coastal sections of the walk (Saxon Shore Way) pass along sea defence embankments of the Swale, Milton Creek, Conyer Creek and Faversham Creek. Beside these waterways are saltmarshes with open tidal mudflats. Many typical saltmarsh flowers grow here, including sea aster, sea lavender, seablite and purslane, with the uncommon golden samphire and sea arrow grass.

The mudflats are rich in small worms, shrimps, marine snails and other molluscs, providing a very rich source of food for birds.

In autumn and winter, large numbers of waders arrive from their northern breeding grounds to shelter and feed in the milder conditions of the Swale estuary. Dunlin, knot, redshank, godwit, curlew and grey plover form part of the flock of wintering birds found on the mudflats here.

The grazing marshes and wet areas provide roosting and feeding grounds for many waders. They are also used by ducks, including teal, shoveler and wigeon, and internationally important numbers of Brent geese arrive in October from Siberia. Eider duck, scoter and red breasted merganser feed in the tidal waters.

The Swale supports more than 50,000 wildfowl and waders during winter.

Winter also brings birds of prey from mainland Europe and Scandinavia which hunt over the marshes and along the dykes for short-tailed field voles and other prey. Hen harriers and short- eared owls are regularly seen from October to March. Marsh harriers now breed in small numbers on the Isle of Sheppey across the Swale and may be seen occasionally throughout the year.

Open lagoons formed in disused clay and gravel pits are found along the walk and in winter, provide shelter and food for many of the ducks from the Swale. In summer great-crested grebe, tufted duck, common tern and black-headed gull breed here and particularly on the old clay pits at Murston.

The drainage dykes vary from fresh to brackish water. In summer a variety of plants grow here, including sea club rush, common reed, water dock, frogbit and lesser water parsnip. Kingfisher often fly along the dykes and mute swan nest in the reed beds. Herons stand on the banks or fish for eels in the dykes whilst snipe are frequently seen on the marsh in winter.

When the dyke and saltmarsh flowers are flourishing, the coast also attracts migrant birds from Africa. These include yellow wagtail which nest in the grazing meadows, often using hoof prints of cattle. Others, including sedge and reed warblers are found in the reed beds with reed bunting, bearded tit and other resident birds. Redshank and lapwing, now in decline as breeding birds, also nest on the marshes.

Stoat and weasel hunt along the sea defence embankments.

Farmland

Much of the inland areas crossed by the Swale Heritage Trail are grazing marsh and orchards. These are well populated by birds of hedgerow and field, such as dunnock, linnet and yellowhammer, with skylarks hovering over the open fields. In winter the orchards, with their fallen fruit, and hawthorn hedgerows with their red berries, are attractive to migrant redwings and fieldfares, arriving from northern Europe.

The Trail also passes by old abandoned industrial workings which have become colonised by hawthorn, blackthorn, wayfaring tree, dog rose and elder with some cherry and apple trees. Wild flowers growing here include wild strawberry, violets, wild mignonette, willowherbs, mellilot, St John's wort, Alexanders and the uncommon Duke of Argyll's tea plant.

The shrubs and bramble provide further rich habitat for breeding birds, and particularly for visiting migrant warblers, including chiffchaff, willow warbler and blackcap, whilst resident yellowhammer, linnet, goldfinch, reed bunting and wren compete for available nesting sites.

Fowley Island

North of Conyer, Fowley Island can be seen offshore. It is now much eroded from its former substantial saltmarsh platform, once home to many hundreds of nesting birds. Today, small colonies of black-headed gulls and a few oystercatchers are found here.

Oare Marshes Nature Reserve

This area of grazing marsh adjoining Faversham Creek is divided by the Harty Ferry Road, which leads from Oare village to the slipway and a small car park. The Swale is used for mooring yachts and fishing boats with the slipway popular for launching small craft.

Overlooking the estuary is the Watch House Information Centre, converted from an old customs outpost. The Centre is open at weekends and Bank Holidays. The Reserve is managed by sensitive grazing and control of water levels to provide pools and reed beds for the benefit of breeding and wintering birds, plants and insects.

Beside the car park is a stand pipe from an old artesian bore hole down into the chalk aquifer deep below the surface. This flows continuously throughout the year and has long been recorded on

the meadow to join Oare Creek. A sluice gate prevents salt water flowing into the meadow. Yellow iris, ragged robin and brooklime can be seen by the dykes.

Ham Marshes

Around Ham Marshes, the Saxon Shore Way coast path provides excellent views of traditional grazing marsh with extensive mudflats and saltmarshes and with further colonies of breeding gulls, redshank and lapwing. Shelduck also breed, often using the shelter of old rabbit burrows.

Hop garden - Gatinstone

shipping charts as a
source of fresh water. It is also a source
of freshwater to the Reserve.

Oare Meadow Nature Reserve

This small wet meadow lies to the south side of the road through Oare. A freshwater stream flows through

INTERESTING FEATURES

The Swale Heritage Trail and Saxon Shore Way run through a variety of surroundings - light industry, sea walls, grazing marsh and orchards. But a hundred years ago the scenery was very different. Much of the land in the Murston, Conyer and Faversham areas was devoted to brickmaking and the creeks were lined with wharves for the sailing barges which carried the bricks to London and elsewhere and returned with cargoes of 'roughstuff' - household wastes incorporated in the bricks - and horse manure for the orchards. The Swale at that time was much less polluted than today and supported oyster fisheries supplying the London markets. The observant walker can still see vestiges of these industries on the route.

1. Murston (old) Church

The little building, surrounded by its churchyard, represents the remains of the original village church, dismantled in 1873-74 when the new village church was built. All that remains of the old church is the central chancel. The church was built in the late-12th or early-13th centuries and was mainly Early English in style. It had a square tower with a wooden turret housing three bells. Its nave had an arcade each side and there were three chancels. Towards the end of the 19th century the church was falling into disrepair and was being badly affected by fumes from the gas works nearby. The rector therefore decided to raise funds to build a new church nearer the centre of the village. Three of the pillars and arches from the old church were incorporated in the new, the old altar stones were installed in the floor of the aisle and one of the bells was hung in the tower. The last interment in the old grave yard took place in 1920.

2. Milton Creek

From Murston church the Saxon Shore Way leads down the slope to the banks of Milton Creek, passing, on the northern side, the site of the old gas works built in 1853. At the foot of the slope is the old Murston Parish Quay and turning north you pass a house which in former times was the Brickmakers Arms. The public house was built by George Smeed, a local brickmaker, in 1859 and must have done a thriving trade with the thirsty bargemen and brickfield workers.

As you follow the path northwards along the side of the creek you may see the remains of numerous sailing barges, abandoned here and burnt out when the heyday of brickmaking ended over 50 years ago. The last surviving brickworks can be seen to the east of the footpath - but this now relies on imported materials and road transport.

3. Oyster Ponds

In the corner formed by the junction of Milton Creek and the Swale, you will see the lakes which were the old oyster rearing ponds. These are now a haven for a wide variety of wildfowl. From here you can see the saltings known as 'The Lilies' at the mouth of the creek and across the other side of the Swale the grazing marshes of the Isle of Sheppey.

4. Meres Court

Meres Court was the smallest of the three manors of Murston. The manor house is timber-framed with the first floor oversailing.

MM House - Tonge

5. East Hall

East Hall Manor was the largest of the three ancient manors of Murston. The manor house dates from the 15th century and has a tithe barn of about the same age. The stock brick extension was built in the mid-19th century. The land round about was excavated for brick earth in the heyday of brickmaking in the last century.

6. Lagoons

North-east of Murston the Saxon Shore Way passes through old brickworking areas and along the sea wall are passed saltmarshes and open lagoons created from old clay pits. These now form a nature reserve.

7. Tonge Castle

The site of Tonge Castle is on the raised ground to the north-east of Tonge Pond, now occupied by a modern bungalow. The castle was protected by ditches, one of which now forms Tonge Pond. Excavations carried out in 1930 revealed the foundations of walls about 14 inches thick. Above these low walls the castle probably had wooden palisade walls. The excavations suggested that the castle was occupied during the 12th and 14th centuries although there were signs of earlier occupation during the 1st century AD.

Legend has it that the castle was built by the Saxon Hengist who had gained the land in the area by a cunning trick. About 450AD Vortigern, the king of Kent, in recognition of the help he had received from the Saxons in defeating the Scots and Picts, granted Hengist as much land as could be covered by an ox-hide. Hengist cut the hide into very thin strips or thongs and by laying them end to end managed to encircle an area of 80 acres. The land enclosed by the circle was given the name Thwange or Thong - a possible derivation of the modern name, Tonge.

8. Tonge Pond

Tonge Pond is fed by a small stream which flows from Thomas à Beckett's Spring near Bapchild. Legend has it that pilgrims on their way to Canterbury were baptised in the stream. About 50 years ago the pond was a popular local 'lido' with a small cafe and boats to hire. In more recent times it has had mixed fortunes, drying out completely in times of prolonged drought. Happily the National Rivers Authority have agreed to pump water into it when the flow from the natural spring fails.

9. Tonge Water Mill

The existing mill was built in 1837 on the site of an ancient mill. The Domsday Book confirms that there has been a mill here for at least 900 years. The tall chimney was built for a steam beam engine which provided standby power, presumably in times of drought when the pond level was low. When the new mill was built in 1837 the old building next door became a bakery. The buildings, which are listed, have in more recent years been converted to private dwellings.

10. St Giles' Church, Tonge

There has been a church on this site since the 12th century. The church is built in Norman and Early English styles, the oldest part being the arcade of four arches to the north of the nave. It dates from 1160. The small 13th-century tower at the west end contains three bells, two dating from 1626 and one from 1784. The fine oak rood screen, of unusual pattern, dates from the 14th or 15th centuries while the font is Norman. In the 19th century a number of frescoes were revealed in the arches by the south door. The best one depicts St Christopher. There are several stained glass memorial windows and in the west window some ancient stained glass. The roof is of tie beam and king-post construction.

11. Elmley Ferry

To the east of the lagoons you will see a track coming down to the Swale, a slipway and a line of posts stretching out into the water. This is the site of the ancient Elmley Ferry which connected the mainland with the west end of the Isle of Sheppey in the days before the first bridge was built at Kingsferry. It can further be identified at low tide, with shingle bars leading out from both shores to meet the tidal channel. Old wrecks by the sea wall show the site even at high tide. Until the 1950s there was a 17th-century ferry house here although the cable-hauled ferry ceased operating about 1940. Its main trade was the transport of sheep and cattle to Sittingbourne market.

12. Chekes Court (Blacketts Road)

This listed building is a classic example of an early-19th- century red brick house. Sited on high ground it has commanding views over the creeks and marshes of Conyer.

SWALE

HERITAGE

TRAIL

CIRCULAR WALKS

ON THE

SAXON SHORE

WAY

ROUTE CARDS &
FOOTPATHS MAPS

SWALE BOROUGH COUNCIL

Kent County Council COUNTRYSIDE

THE ROUTES

The Swale Heritage trail, which runs for $11^1/2$ miles between Murston (Sittingbourne) and Goodnestone (Faversham), links with the Saxon Shore Way at Murston, Conyer, Oare and Faversham forming three circular walks ranging between $4^1/2$ and 10 miles. Linking Public Rights of Way provide opportunities for shorter circular walks.

ROUTE MAP INFORMATION

The route maps are reproduced from the Ordnance Survey Pathfinder Series enlarged to a scale of $3^1/2''$ to 1 mile.

The maps are aligned north/south on all pages. For convenience, the north point and scale appears on the maps.

Maps
Ordnance Survey sheet numbers and titles:

Landranger Series, scale 1:50,000 - $1^1/4''$ to 1 mile
178 The Thames Estuary

Pathfinder Series, scale 1:25,000 - $2^1/2''$ to 1 mile
1194 (TQ 86/96) Sittingbourne
1195 (TR 06/16) Whitstable, Herne Bay & Faversham

Distances and times
The distances and times for each loop are shown on the maps.

WAYMARKING AND SIGNING

The Swale Heritage Trail waymarks are used to show the line of the route in the countryside. You will see them fixed to waymark posts, or posts of gates or stiles. The trail has been waymarked in such a way that it is possible for you to walk the route in either direction. The Swale Heritage Trail logo is incorporated into the different coloured arrows depending on the status of the right of way: yellow for footpath, blue for bridleway or red for byway.

To complete the circular walks follow the relevant section of the Saxon Shore Way.

In most places where the Swale Heritage Trail crosses or leaves a metalled road you will see metal signs fixed to lamp posts or other posts. The logo is added to statutory footpath, bridleway or byway signs, or used on its own where the route follows a section of road.

Changes to the route may occur during the currency of this guidebook, in which case look out for the diversion signs and follow the waymarks.

TRANSPORT

Car Parking

Car parking places are shown on the route maps.
Please note that these are not necessarily car parks.
If a car park is not available, please park
thoughtfully and sensibly to avoid causing an
obstruction or damage to the roadside verges.
Leave your car securely locked with valuables out
of sight.

Bus and Train Service

Bus services operate to Murston, Conyer, Oare,
Faversham and Goodnestone and along the A2
between Sittingbourne and Faversham. Railway
stations are located at Sittingbourne, Teynham and
Faversham on the London (Victoria) to Ramsgate
line.

It is not practical to give details of all bus and train
services to points along the Swale Heritage Trail,
since they may change during the currency of this
guidebook. Kent County Council publishes an
annual public transport map and guide which
contains a comprehensive bus and rail route map
and operators.

For details of train services please telephone either
Tonbridge (01732) 770111 or London 0171-928 5100.

You are advised to check details of your journey
before travelling particularly for Sunday services.
Public transport information countywide can be
obtained from Kent County Council, Highways and
Transportation Department, Springfield, Maidstone,
Kent ME14 2LQ, telephone freefone 0800 696996.

OTHER WALKING OPPORTUNITIES

If you have enjoyed these walks and would like to
explore other waymarked walking routes in Kent,
write to the Access and Recreation Officer (listed
elsewhere) for a publications catalogue. Other
circular walk guidebooks in this series are planned
and in preparation.

It is possible for you to devise your own circular
walks using the extensive rights of way network
throughout the county. Information about these can
be obtained by studying either the Ordnance Survey
Pathfinder maps or the Kent County Council
Definitive Maps of Public Rights of Way. Copies of
the latter can be inspected at public libraries or
district council offices. In the event of difficulty
please contact the Public Rights of Way Manager
(listed elsewhere).

The Swale Heritage Trail links to the Saxon Shore
Way, a 140 mile linear route which traces the old
shore line between Gravesend on the Thames
Estuary and Rye in East Sussex. The name comes
from a series of fortifications built by the Romans to
defend the country against Saxon pirate raids.

Publication:
'Saxon Shore Way Guide in ten sections' - Kent area
of the Ramblers' Association, c/o Mr E Kingstone,
40 Hollywood Lane, Wainscott, Rochester, Kent
ME3 8AL or the KCC Access and Recreation Officer.

KEY TO MAP SYMBOLS

Swale Heritage Trail - fully signed and waymarked

Saxon Shore Way

Optional access points or detours - not waymarked

Other footpaths - not promoted

ZF29 Right of Way number

5 Interesting feature

Railway station

Bus route

P Car parking

Telephone

i Information

WC Toilet

Public house

Pub food

Cafe / restaurant

Foodstore

View point

! Caution - take care

Saxon Shore Way

Aerial Ropeway

Slipway Elmle

ZU1

3

Dug-out Canoe found

Mill

Kemsley Down

Castle Rough

Kemsley Marshes

14

Works

Church Marshes

Milton Creek

ZU1

2

Sewage Works

2

ZU1

Pipe Line

Sch

Hospl

Sch

Liby

Burial Ground

ZU

Wks

ZU1

ZU20

Burial Ground

ZU45A

ZU22

A2

ZU23

SITTINGBOURNE
All facilities

Murston

16

Sch

2

1

ZU3

ZU13

ZU14

T

4

Mere Court

5

ZU16

MURSTON

Burial Ground

Allot Gdns

ZU16

ZR205

Snipshill

N 0   1 Kilometre   1 Mile

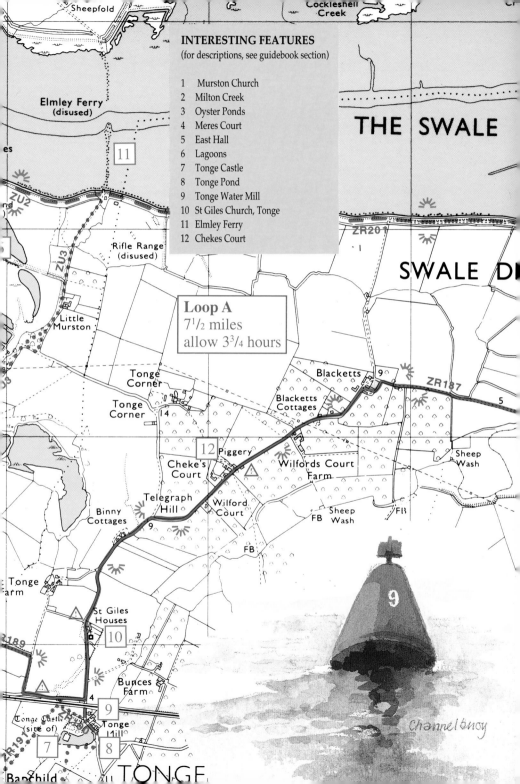

INTERESTING FEATURES

(for descriptions, see guidebook section)

1 Murston Church
2 Milton Creek
3 Oyster Ponds
4 Meres Court
5 East Hall
6 Lagoons
7 Tonge Castle
8 Tonge Pond
9 Tonge Water Mill
10 St Giles Church, Tonge
11 Elmley Ferry
12 Chekes Court

THE SWALE

SWALE D

Loop A
7½ miles
allow 3¾ hours

Sheepfold

Cockleshell Creek

Elmley Ferry
(disused)

11

Rifle Range
(disused)

Little
Murston

ZU2

ZU3

ZR201

ZR20

ZR187

5

Tonge
Corner

Tonge
Corner

Blacketts

Blacketts
Cottages

9

Sheep
Wash

14

12 Piggery

Cheke's
Court

Wilfords Court
Farm

Telegraph
Hill

Wilford
Court

9

Binny
Cottages

FB

Sheep
Wash

FB

FB

Tonge
Farm

St Giles
Houses

10

3189

Bunces
Farm

4

9

Tonge Castle
(site of)

Tonge
Mill

7

8

Bapchild

TONGE

channel buoy

9

E DISTRICT

Loop A

ZR201

13

Fowley
Island

18

South Deep

Wharf

ZS234

2

Conyer Creek

5

ZR187

Wks

The
Firs

ZR309

eep
sh

ZR188

Wks

PH

Conyer

T

CONYER

🚐 🅿 ☎
🍺 ✗ 🍴

4

Dock

ZR198

ZR279

3

⚠

Stone Chimney
Farm

Banks
Farm

ZR241

14

Teynham
Court

9

ZR242

16

Teynham Court
Farm

15

Peete
House

Wks

ZR238

Spr

17

ZR244

Wks

ZR239

ZR243

ZR245

3

⚠

🚉 Sta.

Barrow
Green

Osiers
Farm

Deerton Street
Farm

TEYNHAM

🚐 🅿 ☎ 🏛
✗ 🍴 🎣

Sch

Deerton
Street

Spr

ZR246

Elve

ZR250

ZR251

Whent's
Farm

Nicholl
Farm

BS

19

Church
(remains of)

The Ol
Farmho

(A2)

ZR253

ham

Lower
Newlands

Tumulus

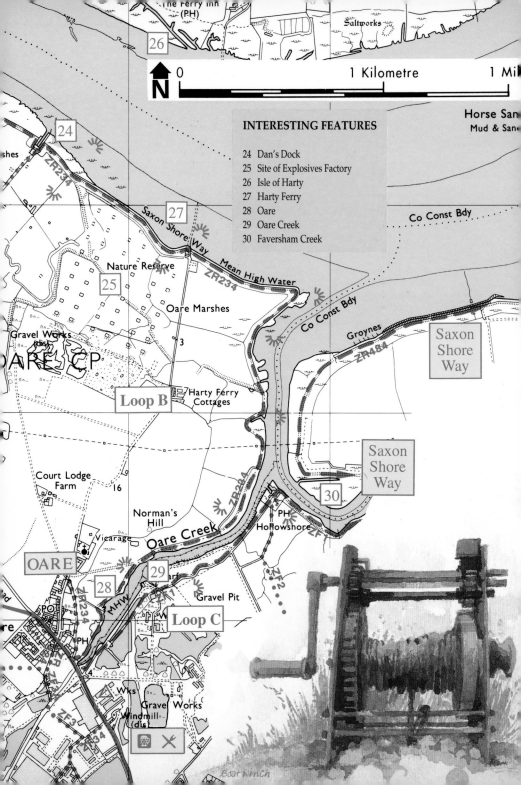

The Ferry Inn (PH)

Saltworks

26

N 0 1 Kilometre 1 Mil

Horse San
Mud & San

24
ZR234

shes

INTERESTING FEATURES

24 Dan's Dock
25 Site of Explosives Factory
26 Isle of Harty
27 Harty Ferry
28 Oare
29 Oare Creek
30 Faversham Creek

Saxon Shore Way

27
ZR234

Mean High Water

Co Const Bdy

Nature Reserve

25

Oare Marshes

Co Const Bdy

Groynes

Saxon Shore Way

ZR484

Gravel Works (dis)

OARE CP

3

Harty Ferry Cottages

Loop B

Saxon Shore Way

Court Lodge Farm

16

30
ZF

Norman's Hill

ZR284

PH Hollowshore

Oare Creek

Vicarage

OARE

29

ZR234

MHW

28

Gravel Pit

Loop C

PO

PH

ZF2

Wks

Grave Works
Windmill (dis)

ZF3

ZF34

Boat Winch

Tourist Information

Faversham: Tourist Information Centre, Fleur de Lis Heritage Centre, 13 Preston Street, Faversham, Kent ME13 8NS, telephone Faversham (01795) 534542.

Sittingbourne: Swale Borough Council, Leisure Services Department, Swale House, East Street, Sittingbourne, Kent ME10 3HT, telephone (01795) 424341

Ramblers' Association, 1/5 Wandsworth Road, London SW8 2XX, telephone 0171-582 6878. Kent Area Secretary: Brian Arguile, 42 Waldron Drive, Loose, Maidstone, Kent ME15 9TH, telephone Maidstone (01622) 744207.

Countryside Commission, South East Regional Office, 4th Floor, 71 Kingsway, London WC2B 6ST, telephone 0171-831 3510.

Ordnance Survey, Romsey Road, Maybush, Southampton, Hants SO9 4DH, telephone Southampton (01703) 792000.

Weather (up to date weather forecast) Kent area 0891 14 12 12

USEFUL ADDRESSES AND/OR TELEPHONE NUMBERS

If you have any comments or suggestions about this or any other recreation route, please contact the Access and Recreation Officer, Planning Department, Kent County Council, Springfield, Maidstone, Kent ME14 2LX, telephone Maidstone (01622) 696168.

The routes should not be obstructed in any way but if they are please contact the Public Rights of Way Manager, Highways and Transportation Department, Kent County Council, Springfield, Maidstone, Kent ME14 2LQ, telephone (01622) 696740.

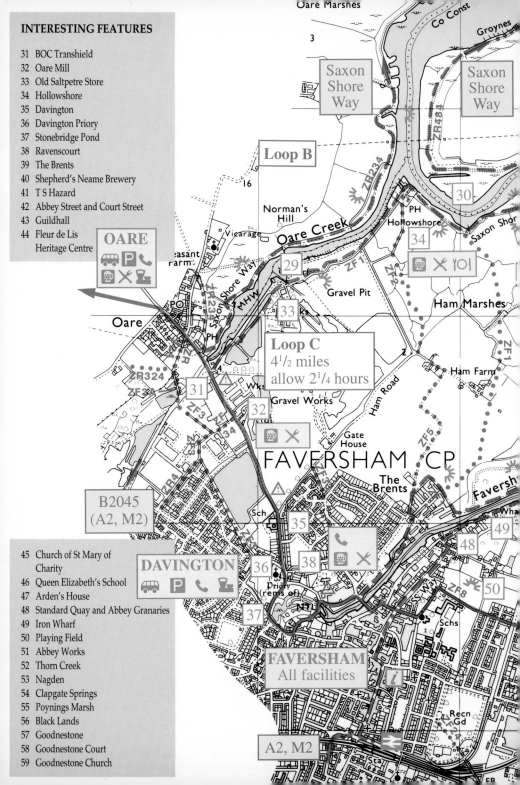

INTERESTING FEATURES

31 BOC Transhield
32 Oare Mill
33 Old Saltpetre Store
34 Hollowshore
35 Davington
36 Davington Priory
37 Stonebridge Pond
38 Ravenscourt
39 The Brents
40 Shepherd's Neame Brewery
41 T S Hazard
42 Abbey Street and Court Street
43 Guildhall
44 Fleur de Lis
   Heritage Centre

45 Church of St Mary of
   Charity
46 Queen Elizabeth's School
47 Arden's House
48 Standard Quay and Abbey Granaries
49 Iron Wharf
50 Playing Field
51 Abbey Works
52 Thorn Creek
53 Nagden
54 Clapgate Springs
55 Poynings Marsh
56 Black Lands
57 Goodnestone
58 Goodnestone Court
59 Goodnestone Church

OARE

DAVINGTON

Loop B

Loop C
4½ miles
allow 2¼ hours

Oare Marshes

Saxon Shore Way

Saxon Shore Way

Norman's Hill

Oare Creek

Hollowshore

Ham Marshes

Gravel Pit

Vicarage

Oare

Gravel Works

Gate House

Ham Road

Ham Farm

FAVERSHAM CP

The Brents

Faversh

B2045 (A2, M2)

A2, M2

FAVERSHAM
All facilities

Priory (rems of)

Recn Gd

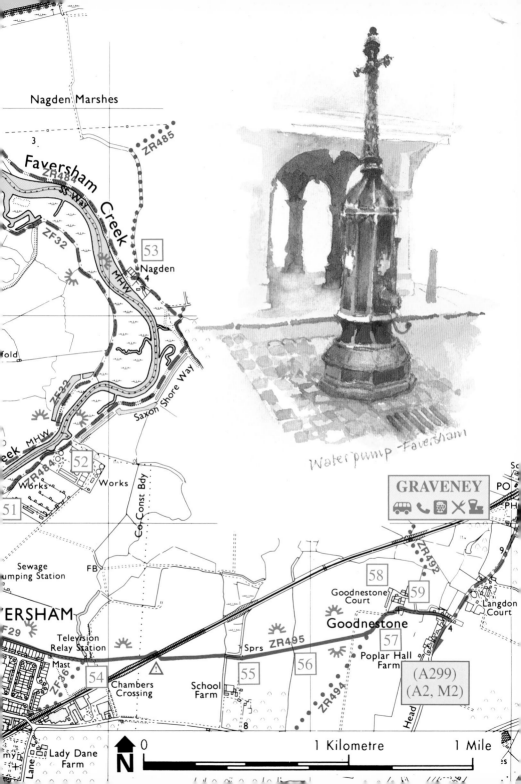

Nagden Marshes

3

ZR485

Faversham Creek

ZR484

SS Way

ZF32

MHW

53

Nagden

4

Saxon Shore Way

ZF32

ZR484

MHW

eek MHW

fold

Works

52

Works

Co Const Bdy

51

Works

Waterpump - Faversham

GRAVENEY

Sc

PO

PH

ZR492

9

Sewage
umping Station

FB

58

Goodnestone
Court

59

Langdon
Court

ERSHAM

ZF29

Television
Relay Station

Goodnestone

57

Poplar Hall
Farm

4

Mast

Sprs

ZR495

55

56

(A299)
(A2, M2)

ZF36

54

Chambers
Crossing

School
Farm

ZR494

Head

8

my

Lane

Lady Dane
Farm

N 0   1 Kilometre   1 Mile

A WALKERS CODE

Remember that most of the public paths cross private estates and farmland. You are walking through a place of work; enjoy the countryside but please show respect for its life and work.

Always keep to the path to avoid trespass, and when faced with growing crops walk in single file.

Remember to leave things as they are - fasten those gates you find closed. Straying stock can cause damage, and inconvenience to farmers. Always use gates and stiles to cross fences and hedges.

Take your litter home with you otherwise it can injure people and animals (including wildlife). Guard against all risk of fire, especially in dry weather. Picnicking is not permitted on private land; you only have a right of passage on a right of way.

To avoid injury or distress to farm animals and wildlife, keep your dogs under control at all times. If not on a lead they can run surprisingly long distances and consequently out of sight of the owner. Farmers have a right to shoot dogs found worrying animals.

Take care when crossing or walking along country roads. Keep to the right in single file facing oncoming traffic. On a bend, however, walk on the outside.

Always wear suitable clothing and footwear for the season. Be prepared for cold and wet weather, in which case take with you clothes which are warm and waterproof. Inexpensive overtrousers will protect you from any discomfort caused by walking through high vegetation or crops after rain. Sections of the path may be muddy after periods of rain so wear strong, comfortable and waterproof footwear.

Allow plenty of time to complete your chosen walk. Reckon on walking 2 to $2^1/2$ miles an hour. Allow more time if it has been wet, if you are elderly or have children or inexperienced walkers with you.

For the very fit and enthusiastic there is the opportunity to walk the entire inland route (Swale Heritage Trail) and return on the coastal route (Saxon Shore Way), or visa-versa. However, it is advisable to be very much less ambitious unless you and anyone you are walking with is accustomed to such long walks and have the appropriate footwear and equipment. Once committed to a long walk there are few opportunities to change your mind. There are, for instance, no public telephone kiosks and no regular bus services along any portion of the trails except within the urban areas and key access points. Please consider the wind chill often experienced on the marshes.

13. Sea walls and Conyer Creek

The sea walls were built after the disastrous floods of 1953. In the brickmaking years of the 19th century Conyer Creek was a bustling little port, filled with sailing barges loading and unloading their cargoes and waiting for the tides to take them out to the Swale. You may still see a barge or two on the creek but the main traffic now is pleasure boats which find a safe haven in these sheltered waters.

14. Archbishop's Palace, Teynham

In about the 8th century the Archbishops of Canterbury were granted the Manor of Teynham in exchange for land in the Cray Valley. They built their palace on a site to the west of the church. The site of the Palace was excavated in 1983 and foundations were found dating from the 12th to 15th centuries. There was evidence that the present church was a major element of the Palace layout. King Henry III is recorded as having stayed at the Palace on a number of occasions around 1230 but in the first half of the 16th century the Palace came into the hands of Henry VIII and was subsequently demolished.

15. St Mary's Church, Teynham

The ancient parish church of St Mary's probably dates from the early-12th century although the tower is probably 15th century. The walls of the church contain quantities of Roman building materials, doubtless pillaged from earlier buildings. Noteworthy features are the organ gallery and the impressive crown-post roof. The massive west door is original, dating from the 15th century, and bears the scars of bullets said to have been fired by Cromwell's Roundheads pursuing Royalists who had taken shelter in the church.

16. Teynham Street

The name Teynham (originally Tenham) may derive from the ten hamlets which formed the parish. In Roman days the geography of the area was much different from what we see today. At that time the waterfront was just behind what is now Teynham Street and vineyards clothed the terraced slopes to the shore line. It is probable that in Norman times sea walls were built which led to the formation of marshes on their landward side. Mosquitoes and the 'ague' (malaria) then became a problem and the inhabitants of the village which had grown up around Teynham Street were forced to move to more healthy areas further inland. They settled along the old Roman road which came to be known as Greenstreet and did not return to the lands nearer the Swale until the problems of the marshes had been overcome in medieval times.

17. North Kent Fruit Belt

The North Kent Fruit Belt, of which this forms part, is world-renowned for its fertility. They may grow bigger, more highly coloured fruit elsewhere, but for flavour not much can beat a Kentish Cox.

18. Fowley Island

The name 'Island' is superfluous, as in old English Fowley means 'bird island'. There are more good views of Sheppey to the west and the east, traces of a disused rifle range.

19. Buckland Farm and St Nicholas' Church

Just south of the Trail lies Buckland Farm, with a fine medieval timber-framed granary and what little remains of St Nicholas' Church. This was badly damaged in a gale in 1706 and it was beyond the means of the very small parish to rebuild it.

20. Elverton

At a right-angle bend is located an 18th-century house which till 1993 was the Mounted Rifleman Public House, where there were no pumps and beer was still served medieval-style by hand from the cellar. In December 1821 the great radical campaigner William Cobbett stayed a couple of nights at nearby Elverton Farm, and was much impressed with local farming practice and productivity:

"As far as soil goes, it is impossible to see a finer country than this. You frequently see a field of 50 acres, level as a die, clean as a garden and as rich. I am now sitting in a room from the window of which I look, first, over a large and level field of rich land, in which the drilled wheat is finely come up, and which is surrounded by clipped quickset hedges with a row of apple trees running by the sides of them; then, over a long succession of rich meadows, the shortest grass upon which will fatten sheep or oxen."

21. Luddenham Gut

The pastures alongside the 'Gut' have been reclaimed from tidal saltings - hence the intricate network of dykes. Many of these drain into an old natural watercourse, Luddenham Gut, which discharges into the Swale at a sluice and marks the boundary between Teynham Level and Luddenham Marshes.

Church of St. Mary the Virgin Teynham

22. 'Hawks and Beetles'

Hawks and Beetles, an attractive old 16th-century farmhouse. No-one is sure about the origin of the name, but hawks and beetles are both tools used in the building trade.

23. Luddenham Court and Church

As so often in remoter parts of Kent, there is no 'village' in this parish, just two or three hamlets, of which this is one. In lay-out it has hardly changed since the middle ages and not much imagination is required to visualise the scene as it might have been centuries ago, busy with the farm workers since displaced by successive waves of mechanisation. Church and Court (manor-house) lie hugger-mugger and their site is superlative - at the very tip of a ridge overlooking marshes which were probably tidal when the area was first settled. The Church, no longer in use, is looked after by the owners of the Court and you cannot get inside. But do not miss the Norman west door or the Roman bricks re-used alongside it. 1,900 years ago, the whole of this rich area was a favourite with Roman settlers, and doubtless there was a villa here or nearby.

24. Dan's Dock

Dan's Dock is a reminder of the explosives industry. It is situated at the end of a long causeway which leads dead straight up to one of the main factory entrances at Uplees. Isaac and Sampson Dan, let it be said, were there before the explosives factory, making bricks at Uplees, and had built the dock for sailing barges loading their cargoes.

25. Site of explosives factory

Most of the land here was reclaimed for the purpose little more than 100 years ago. The first high explosive to be developed was guncotton, and manufacture began here in 1870. As others were introduced - nitroglycerine, cordite and TNT - they were made here. The factory was 'high-tech' and rather like a new town, with its own water supply, generating station and complex network of main services and works tramways.

A price was paid, however, and on 2 April 1916 at least 116 people lost their lives in the Great Explosion - the worst in the history of the UK explosives industry. In a shed about 600 yards from the sea wall about 165 tons of TNT and ammonium nitrate blew up, and the shock was felt as far away as Norwich. Windows were blown out and other damage done across the water in Southend but Faversham, much closer, suffered hardly at all because it was protected from the blast by the Uplees ridge.

All this was at the height of World War I, and production resumed almost immediately. If this sounds surprising, bear in mind that explosives factories consist mainly of a profusion of small buildings, isolated from one another so that in the event of a 'blow' damage is confined.

Production ceased at the end of World War I and almost all the buildings were demolished, some of the timber ones however being 'recycled' as bungalows, garages and sheds in the Faversham area. You can recognise them by their convex corrugated iron roofs.

The marshes became pasture and attracted interesting bird and plant life. As other similar areas in Kent and Essex succumbed to urbanisation, they became quite precious. In the late 1960s the combined efforts of the Faversham Society, English Nature and Kent Trust for Nature Conservation (KTNC) fought off marina proposals which would have ruined the habitat and then in 1983 the Kent Trust bought 170 acres of the site (the rest is in sympathetic ownership). This area is now managed as a nature reserve. It forms part of the Swale Site of Special Scientific Interest (SSSI) which has been formally recognised as a wetland of international importance under the 1973 Ramsar Convention. In an era of reckless urbanisation it may be some compensation that the site of a huge 'high-tech' factory is now a haven for wildlife, and properly protected and managed.

26. Isle of Harty

The Isle of Harty was once separated from the rest of the Isle of Sheppey, by a navigable channel (Capel Fleet). Indeed till medieval times this was used by shipping in preference to the eastern reaches of the Swale - and to this day Harty remains technically part of the mainland hundred of Faversham.

27. Harty Ferry

The road here leads to Faversham and gave access to a ferry which for centuries linked the Kentish mainland with Harty and the rest of eastern Sheppey. Harty, after all, is a delightful spot, with a

Conyer Creek

characterful pub and evocative church, which claims to be the remotest in Kent. These days the long ferry hard is used only by the users of pleasure boats, for whom this is a popular area.

A wonderful sight if you happen to be here at the right time (usually early August) are the old-time vessels which rally here for the annual Swale Smack and Sailing Barge Match. Particularly on a still day, or when ochred sails are spread, the clock really does seem to have been turned back, with these treasures from the past, lovingly cared for by their owners, riding gracefully at anchor.

Attempts are being made to re-establish a regular passenger service across the Swale and are likely to be ready in the summer of 1995.

28. Oare
Below the village of Oare land has been reclaimed and it is not too difficult to visualise how tidal water once lapped at the base of the ridge on which it is built.

It is worth visiting the medieval village church, whose churchyard commands a good view over the marshlands to the east.

29. Oare Creek
The old coastline is marked by an embankment (to the west), under Normans Hill (named doubtless after the Danes who, in the 9th and 10th century, used to settle on Sheppey for the summer and held Kent's coastal areas up to ransom).

30. Faversham Creek
Out in the Swale north-east of here were oyster-beds managed for centuries by the Faversham Oyster Fishery Company, originally a trade guild but now a commercial company, which features in the Guinness Book of Records as the oldest company in the UK.

This creek penetrates much further inland than Oare Creek, and has always been the more important of the two. Indeed without it there would have been neither port nor town of Faversham.

31. BOC Transhield
This big depot is under contract to service Marks & Spencer stores in the South-East and continental Europe. The site of this depot, and of the adjacent Thomas Seager foundry, was once a vast brickfield.

32. Oare Mill
The stump of Oare Mill, which was rebuilt c.1860 after a fire, is now a house. This is why the adjacent Windmill Public House is so named; it was built to quench the thirst of workers in the nearby brickfield.

33. Old Saltpetre Store
The brick building with a convex corrugated iron roof is the old Saltpetre Store, one of the few surviving buildings of another of Faversham's three powder factories, the Marsh Works. Like all the others, this closed in 1934, much of the plant and many of the employees transferring to ICI's factory at Ardeer, in Ayrshire (the company saw the war-clouds gathering and felt that in the event of hostilities, Scotland might be a safer location than Faversham, which is closer to mainland Europe). The Works was the first in the world (in 1847) to produce guncotton.

34. Hollowshore (or Holly Shore)
Holly Shore is situated at the confluence of Oare and Faversham Creeks. It seems an unlikely spot for holly, and none grows there, so possibly this was originally Holy Shore, sanctified for some good reason now long forgotten. Once the site of a active barge-repair yard, it is now active with leisure boats. Tired or thirsty walkers will enjoy a warm

welcome at the Shipwright's Arms, an unspoiled 18th-century public house. Spare a thought for the landlord in 1953, who saw the building flooded to a depth of 14 feet.

35. Davington

On the eastern side of the road are the original Victorian houses of Priory Row, locally known as the 'Forty Thieves' for reasons into which it may be as well not to delve too deeply. At No. 1, a bit improbably, all the plans for the post-war restoration of St Paul's Cathedral and the Sheldonian Theatre, Oxford, were drawn by distinguished architect Walter Godfrey Allen. You can imagine that he bought the house because it was the last place anyone would expect to find him, and he could get on with his intricate work undisturbed.

36. Davington Priory

The priory was founded as a nunnery in 1153. It survived the Reformation because it closed before Henry VIII dissolved the monasteries. The church is austerely moving in its Norman simplicity. The nuns' quarters are now the home of two distinguished media personalities, one (an Irish citizen) awarded a KBE for his efforts to tackle the problem of famine in Africa.

37. Stonebridge Pond

The Pond, you will see, is no ordinary example of its kind - rather an intricate maze of waterways. It was part of the first of the town's three gunpowder factories, and as far as possible the product was moved from process to process by water. Otherwise, a spark from a wagon-wheel or horse's shoe, and .... you can imagine the consequences. Even with these precautions, there was a severe 'blow' on the pond in 1781, so bad that it generated a 'mushroom' cloud which could be seen as far away as Reculver.

Abbey Street - Faversham

38. Ravenscourt

Situated opposite the priory's postern gate, Ravenscourt is a typical Kentish 16th-century timber-framed farmhouse.

39. The Brents

The Brents is Faversham's first Industrial Revolution suburb. Pollocks started building concrete vessels for the Admiralty here in 1917 and by the time they closed in 1970 had built over 2,000 vessels of all types, from lighters to stern-wheelers, from barges to trawlers.

40. Shepherd Neame's Brewery

This is the only major brewery left in Kent and also the oldest in the country.

41. T S Hazard

Built as a town warehouse in the 15th century, and still belonging to the local authority, it now serves as the local Sea Cadet HQ. It takes its name from the ship Faversham supplied to fight the Spanish Armada in 1588.

42. Abbey Street and Court Street

Now recognised as two of the finest medieval streets in the country, these were laid out in the 13th century along a single axis as the spine of a Faversham New Town to complement the Old Town just to the south. The idea was both to form a grand approach to Faversham Abbey and to yield it tenant revenue. The monks chose well, siting the streets on a ridge between the creek and Cooks Ditch, one of its minor tributaries.

Faversham

A member of the Confederation of Cinque Ports, the town is one of the most attractive in the country, with nearly 500 listed buildings, all lovingly cared for.

43. Guildhall

A market has been held under the Guildhall for 400 years. The present Guildhall replaced an Elizabethan market hall in the 19th century, but retained the original oak pillars. Nearby is a decorative Victorian water-pump.

44. Fleur de Lis Heritage Centre

Town trails, and many other publications about the town and surrounding area are available at the Fleur de Lis Heritage Centre, whose wide-ranging museum displays are well worth a visit, in Preston Street. The Centre is run by voluntary effort and all profits are ploughed back for its work for the care of the area.

45. Church of St Mary of Charity

The parish church of St Mary of Charity is the second largest in Kent, after Maidstone. The tower, with its elegant, far-seen spire, is the most modern part of the building. It was completed in 1797 and replaced an earlier tower which had been weakened by successive explosions at the nearby gunpowder factory. To minimise the effects of blast, the new spire was of open-work form. If you are expecting a building which is 100% Gothic, you are in for a big surprise! Make sure you do not miss the 16th-century choir stalls with their misericords (tip-up seats) - they feature vigorous carvings of beasties, mostly mythical, and even, in the bench-end finials, a three-dimensional strip cartoon.

46. Queen Elizabeth's School

Either side of the footpath is the history of education in a nutshell - the 1968 campus of Queen Elizabeth's School to the south east and the original building of 1587 to the north west. Since 1887 this has been used as a Masonic hall but the original first-floor school room remains much as it was 400 years ago.

47. Arden's House

At the northern end of the footpath, where it narrows, is a low stone gateway. It was through this that the murderers of Thomas Arden brought his body in a snowstorm in February 1551. Unfortunately from their point of view, it stopped snowing, their footprints could be traced, and they were soon arrested. In Abbey Place you catch a glimpse of the back of Arden's House, where the crime took place. In 1592 an unknown, but gifted, playwright dramatised the story and 'Arden of Faversham' still holds its place in the repertory. Sometimes it is produced in the garden of the house where the murder actually took place. Arden's House was Faversham Abbey's guest-house, where Cardinal Wolsey, among others, was entertained.

48. Standard Quay and Abbey Granaries

Ranges of evocative tarred and weatherboarded warehouses, behind which are the so-called Abbey Granaries. These are a good example of how timber-framed buildings used to be recycled. Their timbers originally served as the frame for the refectory of Faversham Abbey, then after its dissolution in 1538 were used as a kit of parts for this new warehouse block. The late-Georgian house was the home of John Matthew Goldfinch, one of the town's most famous shipbuilders. One of his sailing barges, though intended only for the waters of the Thames Estuary, successfully made a passage across the Atlantic to Guyana.

49. Iron Wharf

At Iron Wharf, when the Creek was rail-connected, was a great fan of sidings. These days most heavy freight traffic goes by road and the wharf has become a boatyard alongside which lie picturesque old sailing barges. A handsome tall brick warehouse now does duty as offices and a dwelling.

50. Playing Field

No ordinary bit of greensward this; beneath it lies the remains of the vast church of Faversham Abbey, larger than many of our cathedrals. When Henry VIII dissolved the monastery in 1538 the building was promptly flattened and the rubble recycled to strengthen the fortifications of Calais, then still a thoroughbred English town.

Not all of the abbey has gone, however. Across the playing field you can see two 15th-century barns which formed part of the precinct. Further along the path, between you and these barns, was a Roman villa (farmstead), and close to this an earlier Belgic settlement. These early settlers certainly had an eye for good sites, close to navigable water but flood-free.

51. Abbey Works

Abbey Works was opened in 1924 to make high explosives, but now producs explosives-substitutes - carbon dioxide cartridges. The layout, with lots of well-separated small timber sheds, is typical of the industry. Nearby is Chambers' Dock, once a brickfield wharf, where another small tributary, Cooks Ditch, joins the creek.

52. Thorn Creek

Faversham Creek's major tributary, Thorn Creek, tidal till 1843, now discharges only at low water through a valve. Till land reclamation work was undertaken around both creeks, some of it as late as the 19th century, it was a large and well-protected haven for shipping. Faversham's sewage treatment plant is near the confluence of the two creeks.

53. Nagden

Nagden is just a few houses and farm buildings but once had a busy little quay. In summer look out for the sea-lavender which grows in profusion here.

54. Clapgate Springs

Clapgate Springs is an enchanting spot where the water still flows, and in sufficient volume to support a colony of wild watercress, surviving from the days when it was cropped commercially.

55. Poynings Marsh

Poynings Marsh is part of School Farm, just visible about 300 yards away to the south. The Marsh is now bisected by the railway line on a low embankment but imagine it as it was 350 years ago, much closer to salt water and sealed from it only by a sea wall about 300 yards to the north. It takes its name from a local family one of whom (Sir Edward Poynings) was responsible for the notorious Poynings' Law (1494) which, till 1782, made the Irish Parliament subject to the English one. Much of this area, including both the marsh and the farm, formed part of the foundation endowment of Queen Elizabeth's School when it first started in 1527, and have remained in its ownership ever since. More watercress used to be grown in the marsh and its naturalised version still thrives.

56. Black Lands

This area is so called because the soil in parts of it is much darker than the pale brown brickearth which is the norm in these parts. To the north there are good views over to Sandbanks, a hamlet atop a long sandy ridge which extends west to Nagden, on Faversham Creek, and east to Graveney. Bear in mind that much of the low-lying area between Black Lands and Sandbanks once formed tidal waters to which the owners of any Roman villa would have enjoyed convenient access.

57. Goodnestone

Goodnestone is a tiny village whose modest half-a-square mile seems to have been carved out of the parish of Faversham to

Chamber's Wharf – Faversham Creek

gratify the manorial aspirations of some 11th-century country gentleman. He lives today in the name of the settlement he founded - 'Godwin's ton' (village). Church and Court (manor house) are next door to one another, as so often. This is another well-chosen site where the soil is high quality and tidal water once lapped within a stone's throw. 300 yards beyond, along the Faversham-Seasalter road, is the little huddle of buildings which forms the village. Serving as backcloth in the distance is part of the Blean, once a Royal hunting forest and very different from the rest of Kent because it lies on London clay.

58. Goodnestone Court

Goodnestone Court is as well-kept as listed buildings should be but so far saved from over-zealous restoration. This is a 15th- century successor of Godwin's original manor house and in a gable on the left boasts an unusual window whose elaborate tracery is done in wood, not stone. By 1560 it was a farmhouse, as it still is today, and Nicholas Wigmore, the tenant, lived there in considerable comfort. He was growing barley, wheat, peas and beans and kept a flock of sheep whose wool was spun on the premises. At the end of a day's work, he and his family ate off pewter plates and drank home-brewed beer. He and his wife, Mildred, had chairs but their six children had to make do with forms. The parlour where they spent the rest of the evening was well-furnished, with silver, carpets and decent furniture. No Panda cars, no police, however, so in this rather isolated spot Nicholas felt it wise to keep weapons at hand. He had two bows and a sheaf of arrows, daggers, a sword and a hand gun.

59. Goodnestone Church

Goodnestone Church is small, and perched on a little hillock, rather like a Romney Marsh church. It is a serene spot, and in all essentials the scene has

hardly changed for 400 years. Not quite as remote as it seems, however: the railway is only 300 yards away, and the dual carriageway Thanet Way less than half- a-mile.

Modest it may be, but the church is really quite precious. Simple two cell buildings of this kind (nave and chancel, no tower, just a belfry) were put up in their hundreds, or thousands, soon after the Norman Conquest in 1066. The vast majority have since been rebuilt or extended. This one has not. So you can see a church today as it would have been seen by a priest, lord or peasant 900 years ago. Quite a haven, beacon, and bulwark it must have been, when most of us were living in mean little hovels of timber and thatch. Daylighting was improved in the 14th and 15th centuries when glass became cheaper but at least one original narrow Norman window survives, deeply splayed inside to spread its slender shaft of light.

In the churchyard the serried ranks of headstones are worth more than a casual glance: elegantly engraved to a standard which is beyond us now, they recall members of local families, like Minter and Murton, some of whom are still represented in the area today.

COUNTRYSIDE ACCESS CHARTER

YOUR RIGHTS OF WAY ARE

❖ Public footpaths - on foot only.
❖ Bridleways - on foot, horseback and pedal cycle.
❖ Byways - (usually old roads), most 'roads used as public paths' and, of course, public roads - all traffic.

Use maps, signs and waymarks. Ordnance Survey Pathfinder and Landranger maps show most public rights of way.

ON RIGHTS OF WAY YOU CAN

❖ Take a pram, pushchair or wheelchair if practicable.
❖ Take a dog (on a lead or under close control).
❖ Take a short route round an illegal obstruction or remove it sufficiently to get past.

YOU HAVE A RIGHT TO GO FOR RECREATION TO

❖ Public parks and open spaces - on foot.
❖ Most commons near older towns and cities - on foot and sometimes on horseback.
❖ Private land where the owner has a formal agreement with the local authority.

IN ADDITION you can use the following by local or established custom or consent - ask for advice if you are unsure:

❖ Many areas of open country like moorland, fell and coastal areas, especially those of the National Trust, and most commons.
❖ Some woods and forests, especially those owned by the Forestry Commission.
❖ Country parks and picnic sites.
❖ Most beaches.
❖ Towpaths on canals and rivers.
❖ Some land that is being rested from agriculture, where notices allowing access are displayed.
❖ Some private paths and tracks.

Consent sometimes extends to riding horses and pedal cycles.

FOR YOUR INFORMATION

❖ County and metropolitan district councils and London boroughs have a duty to protect, maintain and record rights of way, and hold registers of commons and village greens - report problems you find to them.
❖ Obstructions, dangerous animals, harassment and misleading signs on rights of way are illegal.
❖ If a public path runs along the edge of a field, it must not be ploughed or disturbed.
❖ A public path across a field can be ploughed or disturbed to cultivate a crop, but the surface must be quickly restored and the line of the path made apparent on the ground.
❖ Crops (other than grass) must not be allowed to inconvenience the use of a rights of way, or prevent the line from being apparent on the ground.
❖ Landowners can require you to leave land to which you have no right of access.
❖ Motor vehicles are normally permitted only on roads, byways and some 'roads used as public paths'.
❖ Follow any local bylaws.

AND, WHEREVER YOU GO, FOLLOW THE COUNTRY CODE

Enjoy the countryside and respect its life and work.
Guard against all risk of fire.
Fasten all gates.
Keep your dogs under close control.
Keep to public paths across farmland.
Use gates and stiles to cross fences, hedges and walls.
Leave livestock, crops and machinery alone.
Take your litter home.
Help to keep all water clean.
Protect wildlife, plants and trees.
Take special care on country roads.
Make no unnecessary noise.

This Charter is for practical guidance in England and Wales only. Fuller advice is given in a free booklet 'Out in the Country' available from Countryside Commission Postal Sales, PO Box 124, Walgrave, Northampton NN6 9TL, telephone (01604) 781848. Published with kind permission of the Countryside Commission.

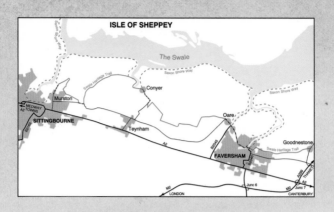

DISCOVER THE PLEASURES OF WALKING IN KENT

The Swale Heritage Trail will enable you to
explore and discover a part of the north Kent
marshes between Sittingbourne and Faversham.

The Swale Heritage Trail (11½ miles) links with the
Saxon Shore Way forming a network of three
circular walks ranging between 4½ and 10 miles.